DRIFT IN
STUMBLE OUT

BY
CASEY HOFFMAN
&
PAUL WEREMECKI

WAIVER

****FOR THE RECORD, WE ARE NOT TO BE HELD RESPONSIBLE FOR ANY GRAMMATICAL ERRORS OR OTHERWISE FOR THE ENTIRITY OF THE BOOK. IT IS 100% LIKELY THAT WE WERE SMOKING WEED WHILE WRITING THIS BOOK.

X_____

ISBN: 9798320139487

Copyright ©*2024*

by Casey Hoffman & Paul Weremecki

First Printing, March 2024

ACKNOWLEDGMENTS

I would like to give thanks to my wife, Laurie Lancaster, who has inspired me through her own work as an author to enable me to be the best version of myself. I would also like to thank my children Paul Jr., Mykala and Saige for their understanding, their growth and their acceptance of my journey. To my aunt Joanne in heaven, thank you for all the lessons you've taught me that have stuck with me through the years on how to be critical of myself in my appearance, my ability to think and my ability to love people with universal acceptance and to love people where they are in this moment in time and not where they came from. To all the naysayers, it is my hope that you can heal your own wounds and move forward as I have done.

I want to thank the spirit of the Drift for being my inspiration and guiding my thoughts during the writing of this book, and the island for being my muse over the years. Thank you to my family and friends who lift me up and encourage me to be my authentic, crazy self and have helped me along my path. Thank you to the entire cast of characters who participated in the making of this book. And here's to us all!

DRIFT-IN AMI

WEEKLY EVENTS!

THURSDAY

Bingo: 1pm - 5pm
Card Games: 530pm - 8pm
Live Music: 9pm - 1am (Dos Macs)

MONDAY

Bingo: 1pm - 5pm
Card Games: 530pm - 8pm
Live Music: 9pm - 1am (Tommy B)

FRIDAY

Live Music: 1pm - 5pm (Dos Macs)
Card Games: 530pm - 8pm
Live Music: 9pm - 1am

TUESDAY

Card Games: 530pm - 8pm
Trivia: 7pm - 9pm
Karaoke: 9pm - 1am

SATURDAY

Live Music: 2pm - 6pm (Outside)
Card Games: 530pm - 8pm
Live Music: 9pm - 1am (Inside)

WEDNESDAY

Bingo: 1pm - 5pm
Card Games: 530pm - 8pm
Live Music: 9pm - 1am (Steve Paradis)

SUNDAY

Live Music: 2pm - 6pm (Tommy B - Outside)
Card Games: 530pm - 8pm
Karaoke: 9pm - 1am

www.driftinami.com

CONTENTS

CHAPTER 1

FOR THE LOVE OF THE DRIFT

There's a host of reasons one would come to the Drift In on Anna Maria Island (AMI), such as to enjoy a frosty cold beverage, to try their hand at karaoke, play bingo or bar fun, perhaps listen to some of the best live music on the island, or meet up with friends. You may even walk out with a potential mate. To say the least, it's not just a bar; it's truly a haven for those who want to shake off the blues, embrace happiness, and let loose on the dance floor. Not to mention those simply passing by happening to look in, just to see what the heck is going on here at this little dive bar everyone seems to love so much.

Judgment-free and welcoming, the Drift In invites you to enter as a stranger and leave as a friend, as Joe Cuervo, the previous owner, would say. "Our wish is to immortalize the legends who have come and gone and to bring recognition to the current status of the World Famous Drift In – AMI." Currently this includes the new owner, staff, customers of old and new, those that are no longer with us and the future legends and friends we have yet to meet. Join us on a journey through the experiences and stories that make this iconic bar a place of laughter and pure fun, ensuring that each page of this book leaves you smiling and reminiscing about the unforgettable moments at the Drift In.

We, Casey and Paul aka Big Sexy, aim to bring you fun stories and survival tips so when you step into the Drift you understand that everyone checks their egos at the door or they don't survive. It is our hope that this iconic bar will live for the next 50-100 years or longer and that patrons will come and enjoy the friendly atmosphere and hopefully become a part of the stories yet to be told! Capturing the World Famous Drift In - AMI is a must for the island and its history and for all the crazy people who love it. It is with our great pleasure and dedicated observations and connection to it, that we bring you first hand into this extraordinary purpose.

Delve into the pages of this book, as it transforms into a tapestry of tales, each thread woven with the vibrant personalities of its patrons. From quirky anecdotes of bingo triumphs to the melodic rhythm of impromptu karaoke nights, we explore the heartbeat of this legendary bar. Many of us have witnessed the evolution of the Drift In's atmosphere through the years. We'll share heartwarming stories of friendships forged over shared laughter and wild dance moves, creating a narrative that mirrors the spirit of the Drift In itself. Get ready to embark on a literary journey where every page unfolds a new chapter of joy, camaraderie, and the indelible mark left by those who embraced it as more than just a bar, but a second home.

As one who documents life and is a lover of the Drift In, I cannot help but want to share my love for this place. I fell in love in more ways than one on Anna Maria Island and the Drift was and is very much a part of my story. For over 15 years, if anyone knew me, they knew there was a likelihood of finding me at the Drift. Maybe not all night, but most definitely a place I would almost always at least stop for one. Which is funny, because you start with one and see where it goes. This place wants what it wants.

Hello! Big Sexy Here! Within this book I will be able to share my experiences and thoughts, while providing some of my fondest memories at a bar that has brought me so much joy, fun, financial gain, and spiritual growth, from my observation of the diversity of people who walk through the doors or sit with me at the tiki bar. Writing this book also allows me to share some insights of the way that I view the world through some of the stories and detailed descriptions of different scenarios that play out there. My hope is to share not only my experiences, but the experience of others for future generations to enjoy as they become patrons of the Drift In AMI..

~

WARNING!

Please do not turn this book into a drinking game. It is not advisable to take a shot every time you read the word Drift because you will be passed out cold in three pages.

So let's dive right in to some favorite toasts to the World Famous Drift In – AMI.

Cheers!

In this dive bar, we raise our glasses not to drown our sorrows but to toast to the the island life, where every sip is a reminder that paradise is found in the simplest of pleasures.

To the dive bar that stands as a testament to our island spirit – resilient, authentic, and always ready for another round of laughter, shenanigans, music and memories.

To our little island oasis, where the drinks are cheap, the stories are rich, and the only thing smoother than the Gulf breeze is the whiskey in our glasses.

CHAPTER 2

DRIFTERS PAST, PRESENT & FUTURE

The Drift In has it mooring lines securely fastened at 120 Bridge Street, on Bradenton Beach, Anna Maria Island, Florida. An anchor point in time since its establishment. This isn't your typical bar; its a living testament to the passage of decades, a nexus of stories, and a sanctuary for those seeking more than just a drink. As we navigate through the pages of this world-famous establishment, let's talk a bit about where we are at on the map.

Anna Maria Island is a barrier island about an hour south of Tampa and is surrounded by four bodies of water. With the Gulf of Mexico to the west, north is Tampa Bay, east is Anna Maria Sound and south is Sarasota Bay. The island has a population of under 7,000 annual residents and attracts nearly 3 million visitors each year from all over the world. While everyone comes here for the pristine beaches, this 7 mile island has everything people could want from an island vacation to island living. With food, music, shopping and fun, it's hard to have a bad time on AMI. There's no trouble finding fun things to do, you can enjoy activities by land or water. Take an island Segway tour, fishing charter, sunset cruise, hire a boat captain, parasail, kayak, bicycle the preserves or even hit the drum circle on Sunday nights at sunset at the Manatee Public Beach. There is no shortage of great places for dining either. You can choose a variety of cuisines from fine dining to old Florida dining at its best and everything from Indian, French, German, Italian, Japanese, Tex Mex and more. The island has over 20 different music venues for you to enjoy. We consider this area a mecca for musicians. Everyone loves being entertained. While most venues are family friendly and allow music til 10 pm, the Drift offers music and dancing until 2 am.

If you are walking down Bridge Street on any given day, no matter who you are, there is a pull to the bar. There's a vibration. Whether its people hanging out chilling or calling bingo, or a typical Saturday with Dos Macs and friends playing out in the parking lot. You'll see anything from a golf carts to Lamborghini's and everything in between. It matters not what walk of life you come from, you can see it all here. The Drift is an "I Love This Bar to Friends in Low Places" kinda joint.

~

The organic nature of the Drift has a sense of poetry in motion. Everybody vibing. It's a good understanding among the locals that what happens at the Drift, gets around. Like herpes, just kidding, or are we... There is no drunk shaming at the Drift, however plenty walks of shame have occurred after a long night partying. But we won't tell on anyone here.

Funny thing about being on an island. It's more acceptable to day drink it seems. Whether you are retired, or just like your happy hour or are visiting and here on island time, the island seems to give permission to let loose a little more than your typical hometown. Sure we could name all the a great establishments, but that's not what this book is about. It's about here, the World Famous Drift In - AMI.

More in it for the recreational games? They have that too! Regulars and visitors make the Drift In a stop weekly for games like bar fun and bingo. Just another reason to put it on the list! And damn straight it is taken seriously. People have been known to leave with hundreds of dollars a game. Hey, it's all in good fun. The point is, as you can see, the Drift In has something for all who love to socialize and have a good time.

How did the it become the world famous Drift In you ask? Owner, Derek Williams, recalls being on vacation with his wife in Ireland. Derek was thirsty for not just a cold one, but for a Bloody Mary. And when it was served up, it sadly did not compare to the ones our dear David Marshall used to make.

Well there just so happened to be some other Americans at this little Irish bar and everyone was chumming up with one another. A lady who was from New York says, "the best Bloody Mary I've had was in Florida." To Derek's surprise, he says "I'm from Florida. Where at? She said Anna Maria Island at The Drift In. They have the best. Derek was beside himself as his wife just happens to be the daughter of Joe Cuervo, the then owner of the Drift. Small world! That's just what the Drift shows you time and again. Whether you go there once and have a most memorable or not so memorable (due to alcohol) experience, the folks you come across at the Drift will continue to remind you that it's a small world. And that is how it became the World Famous Drift In – AMI.

Some of you may remember David Marshall, as his Bloody Mary's were the best around. Not only is David remembered for his cocktail mix, but for his unique look with his long beard and finely decorated hat, he was also great at karaoke as he was known for his amazing voice. And still today Doreen says she will always remember the time David tied himself to the tree that once stood outside the Drift parking in an unsuccessful effort to save

it. Sadly he is no longer with us and would be considered one of the local legends.

It is the goal to show everyone that they are "dive bar worthy" at this establishment.

It's the kind of place you might never drift into on a normal day in your everyday battle of surviving and trying to live your best life in this human construct called the matrix. I want go into details about all that, but that's another book. I guess what I mean to say is; she is no looker. It is a small building painted grey and blue with a very old sign above that says "The World Famous Drift In Tiki Bar." What's awesome is the huge parking lot and the recent edition which is the outdoor tiki bar where I spend many hours bartending and celebrating life as a customer.

The outdoor tiki bar was built in 2013 or 2014 in response to non smokers complaining or walking out. Joe saw the need to give non smokers a place to hang out. Little did he know, the tiki bar paid for itself in less than 30 days as it considerably increased the capacity and profits soared from that day on. This could possibly have been his best business decision other than purchasing the Drift in the first place. And today plans for a new tiki bar are in the works according to Derek Williams, the current owner. As an employee of his I have been directly and inderectly involved in the process of the future of the bar and have witnessed new equipment, new staff, and a new vision which seems to include finding a path forward of keeping the nostaligia, all the while modernizing it to keep up with the evergrowing island. Derek values and supports us as employees and our opinions and needs to enhance the bar. That is something I appreciate very much. I haven't worked for many people like him in my life. It truly is an honor to work at the Drift. Ok as I tend to do, I went off track a bit so let's return.

Making changes to a bar with deep roots amongst the community can present some challenges to an owner, you know because some folks around here hate change. I myself love change and look to it as opportunity and not a defiant act or an act of greed. So many perspectives exist but not all those perspectives are that of the owner of this bar. Successful people like Derek always aim to meet the needs of the majority and not cater to a few. So old timers don't hate the change, embrace it and Derek has your back. He truly understands you and will always try his hardest to meet your needs the best he can. Ok enough about the outside, no wait, we have to talk about the handpainted crooked parking lines, the awesome portable tents that provide shade from the treachery of the blazing sun on an August day in Florida, and the old mural of island life that needs to be recreated or painted over. Dan already called dibs on it. So who the hell is Dan you ask?

Dan is the Operations Manager and is a pretty chill guy who his quite the artist himself. You see, Dan used to be a Psychiatric Nurse in town. From Psych Nurse to Operations Manager of the World Famous Drift In - AMI. I mean hell yes, how else in the world could you have been more prepared. One day you're dealing with psych patients and the next day you're using all that training dealing with the intoxicants at a dive bar. Seems to line up just right if you feel me. Professionally, Dan thrives in this business because of his calm demeanor, his willingness to listen, a desire to want to be better, and his deep understanding of empathy. A good manager may have one, possibly two, of those qualities. He allows us to be who we are while serving customers but he also has his job and responsibilities and has to call you out once in awhile. But the way he calls you out is not in an attacking fashion and I believe people respond well to that. Oh and on a personal note he is just a cool motherfucker navigating his way and trying to live his best life.

So! Let's transition to the inside of the bar. There is no single word that exists that would describe the Drift accurately.

From the outside, if you didn't know, this may look like just an old island dive bar, you'd see some rowdy folks and hear loud music, or maybe catch a scent of cheap perfume and booze. Don't pass this place by! It's timeless. As you cross the threshhold, the hatch door from the tiki bar to the inside, it's as if you go through a portal and get tossed back in time to a scene I could only imagine in an Edgar Allen Poe short story that meets Moby Dick-like characters awaiting your arrival. It's a throw back to a vintage dive bar. The old dark walls, the cigarette tarnished ceiling tiles and the stale, musty smell of cigars and cigarettes. If you look around the place a bit, you'll see "The Babe" memoribilia, memorials of fallen Drift legends, a disco ball, Christmas lights, the Drift In Icon, Mannie and so much more!

I believe it is beacause so many souls have come and gone through the doors, left their mark on the place, and continue to sit in their favorite spots and enjoy the Drift from a different dimension. But they are here in spirit living and loving, like we do all the time at the bar.

Locals come here to gather with family, love, laugh, swap stories, network, make friends, bring guests, and even celebrate life in the present moment. Us locals even argue from time to time. See what people don't understand is how much love there is between family who argue and out here on the Island we are all family. So yeah we get in each others faces and hold one another accountable. But as I say once we process it, it's water under a bridge and we grow through it, not go through it. This truly is a safe space for people to come and chill and air out some grievances knowing that the underlying theme is LOVE. A LOVE for the bar, the island, for belonging, for family, and a sense of community.

~

Currently the owner, Derek, is looking forward to some changes for the vision he sees. He has already made some major improvements to the building and has upgraded a lot of the coolers and making it more effective as a business. Both Derek and Dan believe that as the island evolves, businesses need to as well in order to provide the best customer service, the best experiences for customers and the best business practices.

Let us keep Drifting down memory lane. It's been our observation that customers, employees and locals claim that George Herman Ruth, aka Babe Ruth, once owned this bar. Let's dive deep and see what we can learn.

Big Sexy and I sat down with Joe Cuervo to find out more history from his perspective as a previous owner. Joe purchased the Drift In on Bradenton Beach and the Drift In on Cortez Road around 1995 from previous owner (Ed Shereck). Ed used to tell Joe stories about the Drift.

So legend has it that back in the day, Babe Ruth, most known as the famous baseball player for the Boston Red Sox, New York Yankees, and Boston Braves in a career which ran from 1914 to 1935. In the latter part of his life, Babe would ferry out to the island for the beach and beverages and later he would travel over the original bridge that was built in 1921-1922 that connected the island to the mainland, at the end of Bridge Street. During this time, Bradenton Beach was known as Cortez Beach.

Now back in the day, when the bridge was built, people would drive their old Model T cars across this rickety wooden one lane bridge. When you entered the island you would find that what is today Pines Trailer Park, actually dates back to the 1930's when it was a campground that was used for the likes of the Ringling traveling circus who would winter here in Florida. Since that time, the addition of the bridge made Bridge Street the center of commerce and quite a party spot for Anna Maria Island. The Cortez Bridge was replaced with a more modern concrete structure back in the late 1950's.

Ruth, sometimes known as The Bambino found that what is now the World Famous Drift In-AMI was known by another name, according to Joe, Sit N Sip. Back then, Babe was known for his larger-than-life personality and that he enjoyed a cold beverage. Likely because his father George Sr. owned several saloons in his home town of Baltimore. Sadly his dad lost his life in 1918 attempting to break up a bar brawl.

So one day Babe waltzed into the bar and the owner quickly pointed him out and said you are not welcome here! Babe said do you know who I am? He said yes! Babe asked why and the owner said you came in yesterday and left a bar tab of $3.85. As Babe was leaving, he asked the owner about the for sale sign in the window. The owner said yes it was for sale. So Babe said, I'll buy it! That ought to settle that. He and two Yankees players bought it and owned the bar for about 2 years.

One of our local island friends, David G. said he actually lives in a house that Babe Ruth used to party in with his friends back in the day.

Since that time, other sports players and coaches have enjoyed the likes of the Drift In as well. More recently, Mike Tomlin, head coach for the Pittsburgh Steelers would come in. His drink of choice, as Joe recalls Mike drinks nothing but Hennessy. You'll get the coach from Pittsburgh Pirates and the players enjoying libations at the Drift In. You could find four or five players from the Black Hawks stopping in. Coach Jon Cooper with the Tampa Bay Lightening stops in with his wife from time to time. He's known for liking the Jello Shots.

Cuervo recalls the night Coach came with the Stanley Cup. Coach called Doreen and said he was taking the Cup around the area and wanted to bring it in to celebrate. If you've been around, you know what the deal is, we get to drink out of the Cup! It's a big deal!

Drift-In AMI

According to Wikipedia, The Stanley Cup is the oldest existing trophy to be awarded to a professional sports franchise in North America. It was commissioned in 1892 as the Dominion Hockey Challenge Cup and is named after Lord Stanley of Preston, the Governer-General of Canada.

Obviously Doreen said yes. When the cup was there, word got out. Joe recalls at least 250 people came to the bar just for the occasion, including current owner, Derek who got to drink from it and Big Sexy who was able to touch it but not drink from it. It cost Joe $50 in beer.

Talk about a night to remember!

You shook me all night long! Yeah, you might know the song. This was the first song Brian Johnson wrote as the lead singer for AC/DC. We all know and love his music. Brian also lives in the area and has been known to stop into the Drift In for a beverage. Joe Cuervo recalls the day he first met him. Joe was pulling into the Drift In and noticed a red Ferrari taking up two parking spots outside and as we know, there is limited parking. Joe walks in and asks who's driving this Ferrari? And a little guy, an older gentleman with long hair says that's mine. Joe said can you possibly move it. It's taking up two spots. The guy says nicely sure, no problem. While he was moving the car, the people inside the bar said that's Brian Johnson! Of course, Joe had no idea who the guy was. So when he comes back in, Brian goes over to the jukebox and puts on the song and says that's me singing. I'm Brian Johnson.

Legend has it that even Alabama and possibly Tom Petty

have been spotted there. When asking Joe about other celebrities, he mentioned there is mystery songwriter who comes in who wrote forty percent of Garth Brooks songs. So you just never know who you may be sitting next to at the World Famous Drift In-AMI. We look forward to the day when Garth comes by the Drift to sing a couple songs about the best dive bar.

Now that we've Drifted with Joe, the legend of the Drift story continues with Derek and his staff.

Derek Williams is today's owner of the bar, along with his wife, Helena. She is daughter to Joe and Angie Cuervo. And the time came when Joe was in need of passing the torch, Derek was the perfect choice to further the legacy.

Derek is born and raised in Manatee County and has been a business owner here for years. He and Helena have deep rooted ties in the community and are pretty entrenched in west Bradenton and Cortez. Whether it was a bar or a barber shop, having a business out here was important to Derek. He and his wife have had a lot of good fortune and successful careers and they are thankful they were able to take ownership of the bar as they really want it to stay in the community. What Derek is most interested in is to keep it good, spirited and real. According to our interview with Derek, he stated in this very order. First and foremost he bought the bar to keep it the way that it is. He did not buy the bar to develop it and put a brand new shiny building here. He says while he and his wife own this bar it's not going to be torn down. The authenticity is important to them. That being said, there is a lot happening. Since the tiki was built, both bars have their own personalities. Derek replaced the tents and tables outside. The inside of the Drift they will try to change it as little as possible with changes to mainly electrical and plumbing, etc. The outside bar Derek has a vision of giving it a much different feel. Originally when it was built, it wasn't comfortable even for the people who work there. That doesn't mean new and shiny, but it needs updating and kept with the times. They are paying attention to everything that's also happening around the area on Bradenton Beach as they want to be able to fit in without fitting in so to speak. It's not totally set in stone about how its going to look but that's why they talk to other business owners and go to meetings to stay up to date on the changes and how businesses are seeing the future of Bradenton Beach. Bridge Street will definitely look different over the next decade.

CHAPTER 3

A Fresh Start – Casey's Story

Imagine growing up on dirt roads and small towns, farmland as far as the eye could see. Oh how I dreamed of a place where I could sit at the edge of the ocean with a drink in my hand. Actually my mantra was "I love the feeling of sand in my toes. Me in a comfortable chair, got a great book, sun shining down. Beautiful view of the ocean in front of my eyes." Me. A girl from Kansas. I lived my early adult years dreaming of places far from home. From the books I read to the people I met along my journeys and palm trees were in my mind for as long as I can remember.

Where I come from, smack dab in the middle of the country, there wasn't a lot of choices for live music and dining alfresco. And that's a simple thing this newly free girl wanted. I thought someplace like my mantra would be a good start to the next era in my life. Funny isn't it. I wasn't asking for much. Just a major change of scenery, for the better.

In 2009 I was at a point in my life where I was making drastic changes. After a 9 year marriage and no kids, I wanted to do something different with my life. The sky's the limit! I used to always feel this saying where I came from..."No dreamers allowed." And I was at a place where I wanted to learn about myself and have new experiences. I was finding myself around new people who were actually happy. Living their best lives. I thought, hey if they can do it, so can I!

First I started with reprogramming and getting my mind right. I say this because I had a lot of limiting beliefs and fear. I didn't want to carry those things into my next chapter. Then I got to choose where I wanted to spend the next so many years of my life. At the time, Tim McGraw had the popular song, "My Next 30 Years" and I was turning 30 that year, so it meant a lot to me. Like what did I want to do? Where did I want to live?

To this day, over 15 years later, I still tell the story of picking a spot on the map, just wanting to live somewhere near the water for a time in my life. I chose

Florida as a place to start and one of my mentors said if you are moving there, to check out the west coast as I may like it better. So I lined up interviews from Tampa to Sarasota, with no contacts, having never been there. And when researching I kept coming to the Pier in St. Petersburg. So I envisioned what life could be like there. I told my family I was leaving town. Kansas just couldn't contain me and like I've always said, you can't contain cool! I wanted a fresh start; a new adventure. I had all the things I needed, which were a new laptop, a GPS, (in 2009 it was cool to have a Garmin to get me where I wanted to travel back before Google Maps). I had only clothing, books and the bare necessities that I could fit in my car. And there I was, 29 years old, a Toyota Camry packed to the brim and off to Florida in search of the vision I had, certain that this was a good choice.

Now you could see where I had a few people concerned. Namely my family. I might have seemed crazy, but it seems to have always worked for me. I remember saying to my family, just have a mustard seed of faith that I can do this. I did exactly as planned. I would drive to St Pete and find a place to stay. Go to interviews and see where I land. No real preference. Just close to the water.

I landed a job in Bradenton and it was recommended since I was new to the area to check out Anna Maria Island. So my first Saturday, I woke up and took that drive in search of my new life.

As I was driving looking for places to stay, I came across this little cottage with a for rent sign and a 60 something woman in a bikini wearing a cowboy hat, working in the yard. I got the number and found a place to park near the BeachHouse where I made the call. She answered. Betty Cole La Pietra invited me to meet her in her courtyard where we could visit about that rental.

I arrived and we sat outside introducing ourselves to each other and feeling like instant friends. She agreed to rent me a little one bedroom cottage. Since I had never even laid eyes on where I was at, she suggested I walk across the street to the beach.

Mind you, I had never seen what I was about to see, outside of a couple cruises and a trip to Cabo. I had been to Galveston, and you know the water there…not quite the same.

It was April 2009, I walked 50 steps across the street to the beach on Anna Maria Island. I had no idea! It was a turquoise, crystal clear water kinda day. Absolutely perfect. I'm like, God! What a gift. Truly. It couldn't have been a more benevolent outcome. After about 20 minutes of enjoying the entire feeling of being safe, with a new apartment, a new friend, a new job. Pure Potentiality. Betty walks up, sits down next me and says you didn't know you just landed in paradise, did you honey? She was right. I had no idea where I actually was on the map. I certainly had no idea what I was about to experience.

Betty and I became fast friends. Soul sisters really. Some may remember her fondly as she has been on Anna Maria Island for over 20 years and still is, hopefully til the day she dies. That's her plan anyway.

The cool thing was, Betty knew everything that was going on all week. She knew what I was looking for, live music and outdoor dining. I loved that her and I were both single. We had the time and we found we both loved many of the same things. It couldn't have been any more perfect. And one thing that really drew us close where that we were both from the similar area. She was from Kansas City. I was from west of Wichita.

The first weekend here, Betty had the itinerary set. First stop Tiny's on Longboat Key. She always enjoyed going where single men were. After all, you have to put yourself out there if you are going to meet anyone. That night, we drove back across Longboat Pass, up through Coquina Beach, to the roundabout on Bridge Street, in her 7 series BMW, feeling all excited and new seeing how lively the street was. Now this is 2009, so taking that turn onto Bridge Street on the right, where the new hotel is going in, was the little Italian restaurant.

Interesting that building has had such strange energy over the years. Anyone who has talked to me about that building has said it's always been that way. Strange energy. Nothing ever seemed to work there. Maybe since they are tearing it down to start over with a new resort, they should sage that land for better results. Clear the energy. I digress.

On the other side of the street where Island Time Bar and Grill is today, was an all but empty parking garage with red lights. It would later come to me to be affectionately called the Red Room.

Up until Island Time Bar and Grill opened, the ground floor was pretty much unused. Since I lived just a 10 minute walk up the street, it was no surprise you could find me there after a fun night at the Drift to dance under the red lights. So I like to think I put my energy into that place. Wouldn't you know that the same space I used to dance in is now the space we all dance in at Island Time to some of our favorite bands today, like Bradentucky Death Rays.

Driving further down Bridge Street. She says we must go to the Drift In. That there is a great band playing and we will love it. So we did just that. As we were walking in, Betty said, just be yourself and you'll have a great time. Say no more, we walked through the front door to a packed dance floor to the song of Bobby McGee, sung by Rhonda Hammers, who was playing with the band Hammers and Adams. Betty knew a couple people in there. So she ordered drinks for us at the bar and introduced me to her friends.

Wouldn't you know that every song that night was dance-able? Everyone loved the music. And so many people were moving to the rhythm. This is my kind of place! You know that dance floor is so small, but who cares! We can fit! For the next several months, that band became my favorite band, and we were able to see them every Thursday and Friday. It quickly became my hang out. I learned as I came to live on Anna Maria Island that you may go many places, but you will almost always end at the Drift. A great place for a nightcap, for making friends, for dancing, and feeling like you are no stranger. I think that's what I came to love so much about the island as a whole, when I made the choice not to feel like a stranger. I learned that when you move somewhere, especially by yourself, if you want to meet people, you cannot be shy. Rest assured that this is a place you never have to be shy. No matter what night of the week you go there, no matter what time of the day of the week you go, you will likely never go and not have an experience.

It's clear the Drift has its own plan for you. You could go there with any idea in mind or in any particular mood, and it's expecting you. Nearly every time, you will have left elevated in more ways than one. Needless to say, I got exactly what I wanted, live music and dining alfresco.

It seemed like such an epic time. I was absolutely in love with the island, I was getting so tan, I was cocoa mocho. I was having the time of my life meeting people, having new experiences. I was dating for the first time in my adult life. Met a few of those guys here at the Drift, including one that later became a life partner. Which is funny because one night partying there, a friend of mine said to me, "You are never going to find a good partner here. You gotta go off the island to meet a quality man." I had hoped he was wrong. I figured that if I was to meet someone, the Universe would meet me where I was. And wouldn't you know…

Betty and I would say that we danced the soles off many of our shoes at the Drift In. I sure would love to see that footage they have of us at the Drift. Those cameras sure could tell a story. As they say what goes on at the Drift… well it definitely doesn't stay at the Drift. LOL! I have had some of the best conversations and crazy situations at this little hole in the wall.

Fast forward as a couple years go by and the island is my new stomping grounds and the Drift is my favorite local hometown bar. Especially as a single person, it's great to have your hometown bar. A place you can feel safe going, knowing you will likely meet some fun people and see some newly familiar faces. You will always know a Bartender. And you are sure to know Doreen.

The thing about the island is there is no shortage of fun things to do. And for me, one of the best parts about living in this area is that there is live entertainment every night of the week. There is no reason for any person to ever be bored here. Remember as a girl from Kansas, life could seem like the epic of the quotidian.

I came to know one of the great loves of my life at the Drift. This man, Robert Herman from time to time could be found hanging out there as well. A Long Island man, himself, would find that after traveling all of Florida, that Anna Maria Island was the essence of Florida; the best choice. He was the kind of guy who would take a day off from work at the office in the Bronx, actually call in sick just to book a flight to Tampa, Rent-A-Car and drive straight to the Rod N Reel pier for a grouper sandwich, sit outside and talk to the fisherman, all the while getting a sunburn. Then just a quick flight back to Islip for work the next day. The red face was a telltale sign that the man wasn't sick. You see, that's what island can do to you.

One of his regular nights at the Drift, I was there with Betty, of course enjoying the live music. You know it's hard enough to get to the ladies room when the bar is packed. You got a shimmy and shake just to get through that narrow passageway and hope there's not a line at the door. On this particular night, Robert and Joe, a friend of his, were right at that narrow gate acting as a tollbooth and of course, ladies had to "pay the toll." You can find shenanigans like this regularly at the Drift. I enjoyed playing along each time I passed by with a little shimmy for his enjoyment and mine of course. It was always fun to be playful, but he was over 20 years older than me and so I thought I would just leave it at that.

Somewhere around January 2010, Betty and I were driving her BMW down to the Drift, this time I was her driver, we were having a conversation about my luck with men, since I had only been single a short while. Everything I was doing was not working. I told her I was giving men a break for three months. It was time for me to get more clear, I was loving a beach bum kind of life, looking for my next greatest adventure and trying to find a job at that. Oh yeah, I found out I couldn't have a real serious job because I liked to have too much fun. The island does that to you. It brings out the kid in you. That kid I don't remember being when I was younger. I found over the years that Anna Maria Island was so much fun, that even one day I called in sick from my job to take a cruise with new friends on a catamaran, only to come in to work the next day all nice and tan and got fired! They were actually going to let me go the day before, but as I said, island fun kept me away. So, I learned about being a beach bum for about six months, as I really didn't want just a regular j.o.b. I wanted what my soul was calling for. I wanted to have fun. Be creative, to live fully. But what was it gonna be? What was in store? All I can tell you is that I spent many a day walking the island, riding my bike, laying on the beach listening to Kenny singing Beer in Mexico, looking and waiting for what was to come next in my life.

Then one day, a friend offered me a job becoming a

Segway tour guide. Now this was right up my alley! A fun job. The kind of job a girl like me would like. And it's funny because in my teenage years, I took a trip to Europe and I had the best tour guide! I had this thought that I carried with me for years that if I ever had the chance, I would want to do what she does. And wouldn't you know...Today I happen to own this Segway tour company where we do guided tours of Anna Maria Island and Downtown Bradenton. If you haven't already taken our island tour, well put it on the list as I like to say! We have the best tours you can get, guided by yours truly. Check out ZegwayByTheBay.com for details! OK back to the story.

It was that very night that I swore off men, when Robert asked me on a date and crazy me, I agreed. After our first date of sharing a bottle of wine on the beach at night under the stars, we were rarely apart. Over the next several months, many ideas came about as our relationship grew. He always had a way of one-upping me. And with that, he took my idea of an island newsletter I called the "Sugar Shoes Report", highlighting all fun things and people on Anna Maria

Island, and scratched a business plan in the sand for a radio station. Thus began AMI Radio. He said if we can put it on paper, we can put it on the air! So we created a live streaming and AM radio station. We featured independent artists original music, classical to heavy metal, and a variety of weekly shows. We found that with so much live music in the area, so many of these artists original work was going unnoticed. We wanted to give them a platform for their original work. Through this venture, we found that Manatee and Sarasota counties were a mecca for musicians and amazing talent and our job was to showcase them.

Several of those artists have been known to play or sit in at the World Famous Drift In - AMI. Now, many of you know that it is only a select group of musicians that get the honor of playing in this little dive bar. Over the years, at the Drift alone, we have seen Hammers and Adams to Cabana Dogs to Concrete Edgar and Zack Yoder Band. Solo artists, like Tommy B, Steve Paradis, Dos Macs, Rob Hamm and many others. You never knew who was going to stop by to sit in on any given night. Talented musicians like Koko Ray, Dana Cohen, aka DCX, Steve

Arvey, June Eysel, Brian Blaine, Will Scott, Doug Bidwell to name a few.

AMI Radio had its station at 105 Bridge Street where the old Magnolia Inn was. Between us and our radio show hosts Tim (Hammer) Thompson and Koko Ray, the Drift was a place we could stop before, during or after a show at the station. That's where I first began calling it our living room. It really was and still is! We would all meet there for one, socialize with locals, friends and visitors.

In December 2017 Robert passed, leaving me the radio station and Segway company. It was up to me to decide how I wanted to go forward. It took me a few years to get my bearings. I was unable to continue the AMI Radio endeavor as one could imagine it takes a strong team to sustain.

Sometime later, I was introduced to some crazy islanders who wanted to start a podcast at the Drift and was invited to participate in a live streaming show. Right up my alley, I thought. Next thing you know, we are doing a live show at the Drift In! Showcasing music and talent, businesses and shenanigans. I couldn't help but want to be a part as

I'm a fun girl with the know how to make this happen and I really enjoyed the involvement it gave me. It put me back into a community when for a while I had felt a bit unsure of where my media skills would take me after the station. Long story short, Real Island TV was born. It contained at any given time a host of hilarious islanders, all of whom were Drift Family. Dick, Abigail, Brian, Jill, Patty, Dana, Doug, Laurie and of course Big Sexy along with many "Real Island Friends". You can watch several of our skits, shenanigans and news updates at RealIslandTV.com.

Now, you can still find many of our cast, friends and locals stopping by for a chat at our Drift In Stumble Out Live Show that will be streaming weekly. If you have a story you'd like to share, come and be our guest. It's a show anyone who loves the Drift and Anna Maria Island can watch or listen to live in person or at home wherever you are in the world! We promise you won't want to miss it. Again, you can find out about this show and others by visiting the Drift In Stumble Out, Real Island TV and Drift In - AMI website or social pages.

As you can see, over the years, my relationship to the island has evolved. I feel such a pull to promote it and help to tell the stories in a fun and unique way. The Drift is surely one of the staples in my island life. It's been my living room and at times our stage. It's my hometown bar and my stompin grounds. So when you see me, let's have a toast together. Here's to the Drift!

CHAPTER 4

A Place to Heal – Big Sexy's Story

I would be lying if I said I could remember my first time at the Drift In on the beautiful Anna Maria Island or every memory I have of being there, but that is why I think this chapter will be so intriguing to you as I paint a picture like Picasso for me to share some of my favorite memories as a patron and now a Bartender.

I moved to the downtown Bradenton area in October of 2020 in pursuit of a more healthy lifestyle and the love of my life (Laurie). I was plagued with some health issues related to some complex autoimmune disease, questioning my career as a teacher, and building myself back from a previous marriage. I made the decision to leave all that I knew and take a chance, pursue love, seek a more healthy way of life, and to dive deep into who I was as a man.

The move to Bradenton was very tough on me in the

beginning because I had no family or friends in the area and I was still teaching Physical Education an hour north in Palm Harbor, FL. Little did I know this was exactly what I needed to focus on myself in order to get healthier mentally, physically, spiritually and socially. This is where my angel, my best friend, and also happens to be my wife, comes into play. She stood by me through some very tough times and many hospital stays as we built a solid foundation for our love and relationship which stands stronger than ever.

Soon after the move around four months in I found myself in a wierd place mentally. Anyone who knows me would tell you I don't do depression at all. But I told Laurie we have to make some changes both in the space we lived in and our social status. So we changed our apartment into the coolest, most surreal space anyone could imagine. I love the circus. So we decorated our living room in a twenties style vintage circus tent with some very intricate details, and painted our bedroom a medievil castle where day after day we enjoyed our space and our love grew fonder and deeper.

Now that our space and relationship were flourishing, it was time to move on to stepping up our social game. First it is no secret to anyone that I am a big personality and a very social individual who thrives in communities of free spirits. Fun fact, at my core, growing up and throughout a good part of my life, I was very shy because I had a shame wound from early childhood traumas.

However, I have always believed in universal love and acceptance of all people so it is no secret that I love to get out a lot. At this point, as a couple we were failing to grow socially and it was having a profound impact on my mental health. I found myself bored and a bit depressed because this was unfamiliar water to me. An unhealthy social life that is. Laurie on the other hand is quite the opposite and thrives in solitude. The first eight years of my life I was in and out of foster homes before my loving aunt Joanne and uncle Fred took me in and raised me as one of their own despite my aunt having three children of her own, Ann, Larry, and Vicky. My aunt and uncle also took in my two sisters Roseanne and Tina as well as my cousins John and Diane at times.

As time and the school year went on I was really comtemplating making some serious decisions career wise. It was pretty obvious to myself and others that the last few years of teaching I was loving it less and less due to the role of politics and bias policies that were saturating schools. I felt I could no longer be a part of the indoctrination process. Schools currently have lost many social components and become an institution of division and hate amongst students and teachers alike.

The Trump era really caused alot of divide and it was evident between students and staff members. Whether you supported Trump or didn't, the media blitz and its fancy programmers were reshaping the country and tearing people apart. Ok, I won't get on a soap box or give you my political affiliation because quite frankly it shouldn't matter.

Laurie and I discussed our future plans and our dreams and I reached a decision to get a bartending job out on Anna Maria Island. Sometime around April 2021, I filled out an application at the BeachHouse Restaurant in Bradenton Beach where I was hired on the spot. I had some bartending experience but I had a lot to learn and this was the place to get it.

Working at the BeachHouse was amazing and I served thousands of customers and always enjoyed every shift. The management was top notch and always willing to work with me when I would get sick or get hospitalized. I worked my ass off to be the best Bartender that I could be as I knew this was the beginning of a new evolution in my life.

This is where "Big Sexy" really came alive, a character I created many years ago as a way to embrace my flaws and get others to look past them and not be so judgemental and accept me for who I am.

I remember so many awesome times at the BeachHouse but none greater than the times I spent with Doug Carbee. He is gone now and he will be missed. Love you brother. Doug and I were the two older guys living their best life bartending on the beach with a mutimillion dollar view. We had a lot in common and he pushed me to be a better Bartender. It was some time in June or July of 2023 I decided to leave the BeachHouse and begin working at the best bar ever!

Hold on! You might want to get ready and grab your snorkel as we deep dive into the World Famous Drift In - AMI and the stories I can recall as a customer and now a Bartender.

I'll start by saying I had my eyes on working at the Drift ever since I stepped foot in the bar the first time. There was an energy pull I have never felt in my life. Everytime I am there I feel a sense of belonging. It fills my veins and radiates mirroring my vibration. I have never had a bad time there.

To recall any specifics about my first time at this establishment would be impossible. What is awesome, is my perspective as both customer and Bartender, where I hope to shed some light on just how special the place is.

When Laurie and I decided to work on our social relationships in 2020 we embarked on a trip to Bridge Street. For the record, Laurie had been to the Drift before and I had not. From time to time, we would go and enjoy a few cocktails. We began meeting people from different walks of life. It was immediately evident that this place was special. This is where we would begin to build our empire. It's a place where with every sunrise comes new hope, a saying that brings me back to the foster home days where every morning I would look out the window and repeat that statement in hopes to one day find my way home. That's my empire – that's Anna Maria Island.

Now let's jump aboard the Big Sexy Express – Choo Choo!

If you haven't met me, Big Sexy is the social embodiment of who I am. He is a character created through years of trauma, mistakes, self reflections, education, spiritual growth and so much more. It is no secret after sitting with me enjoying a cocktail, we may just find ourselves swinging from the trapese in philosophy, laughing like the clowns with bar humor, or we might even roar like lions at one another. Come get to know me.

I once wrote "He who acquires the most personalities will return home with most knowledge."

In order to make the transisition from Paul to Big Sexy there is an accumulation of events that must occur so I can rise above who I am at my core, a shy little boy, to bring you a Bartender with a big personality who prides himself on making connections and concoctions like the SexySpresso or the SexySangria for as many customers as I can all the while being the best dive bar worthy Bartender around.

Here's where I want to start with the Big Sexy Express. It's a process. You know, I get up that day, it's different than the day before. I wake up as Big Sexy when yesterday I was just Paul. Clearly, because I have to work today. I like to live like I'm on vacation but the voice inside of me says "Yo bro, this isn't work, this is living." I know I am living my best life and that is why I constantly remind myself I'm not going to work, I'm just living. Truth be told, I'm having the time of my life. But like everyone else, I have to get myself ready for the big dance, the big event or for some, just go to work.

The Drift In, it's my stage. It's my platform. It's where I fulfill my social and intellectual requirements. This is where I become the ringleader at the circus. At least, that's my state of mind. It's the spiritual component that lets you know you are doing what you need to be doing in this moment and it's right. Then I look at the time (and only because it's a workday do I look at the time) and I'm like, Man! I have three hours to do some cool shit before I go play in the circus. So I like to spend some time with the wifey. Maybe have a nice breakfast, go on a bike ride, go to the beach. This helps my mental health immensely.

Now the outfit is next. This is an important step in my process. We switch to "Miva Mode" aka man Diva. Sorta where Janis Joplin meets the band LMFAO (I'm sexy and I know it.) I put on my finest eclectic attire for shorts and a Drift In crew member shirt. I take pride in the fact that I'm not bald yet and that I had the patience to grow out my dreadlocks. So choosing the right hair product for the day has to be made with whether to wear a hat or not, and what hat? These are tough questions that need answering before I get ready. No matter what, the dreads gotta be on point. Continuing on down the list of beautification comes the wide assortment of sunglasses in which to choose from. Do I go with the third eye lenses or do I go with the tortoise shades? These are an important accessory to understanding my divine feminine energy, but don't let that fool you fellas. This patchouli scented alpha male understands what it takes to be the leader of the pack. Upon arrival, it's on! This is my arena for night. I then arrive at my circus tent at the Drift, where I am the clown for entertaining, the sideshow freak for the haters, the lion tamer in case a fight happens, and most importantly the ringleader as Bartender.

It's now time to ride caboose because we are taking you on a fun filled journey of some of our best times at the Drift. So let's goooo!

CHAPTER 5

AS THE BAR STOOL TURNS

PARADISE DWELLERS

A question I often ask myself is however did I find this place or rather how did it find me? I think that is a sentiment that is shared by many patrons when they leave the bar.

Now for most folks, it is the feeling of community and acceptance when you first walk in that is so inviting. For others their first impression could be this is the worst place I've ever seen, but shit I gotta go see what it's all about.

Let's give you an introduction to how this goes. Order at the bar. Pay cash and don't fuck around! Easy as that. It doesn't matter who you are and you never know who you are talking to. You could be sitting next to two people looking exactly the same and one comes from wealth and the other doesn't. The person sitting next to you may be living over at hobo harbor or in a mini mansion on the beach.

For those new to the area, locals affectionately call it hobo harbor, right off the Bradenton Beach city pier. Some looking to live creatively can live "on the hook" as they say right here in the bay. No charge either, though they must have a registered vessel. Now this isn't your typical way of living, but for some, it is a way of life and much more affordable today.

Whether they work at your favorite restaurant just stopping in for a night cap or the coach of Tampa Bay Lightening who recently brought in the Stanley Cup! Perhaps a famous actor or musician, or just your everyday Joe. And the cool factor is that it doesn't matter. Everyone is there for the atmosphere and experience.

Sitting around the bar or outside at the tiki, there could be a real estate transaction, a couple local fisherman talking catch of the day. A group of bridesmaids celebrating. Then of course the whole wedding party, everybody taking shots and taking turns "movin to the groovin." The ones that love this bar, love it for a reason.

There's a lot of stooges and there are a lot of quality

mother fuckers too. That's what makes the Drift such a beautiful place. It truly is unique. You could see the richest dudes there drinking Busch Light in a camouflage can and a poor dude that's drinking an apple martini. Why? Because the price is just right for everybody. That's right, the Drift is known for having the best prices in alcohol on Anna Maria Island!

It doesn't matter. You can be who you are. That rich dude knows he came from somewhere. That's why he's drinking a Busch Light. The poor guy drinking the martini is a guy who was born into money, or he forgot where he came from, one of the two. You drink Busch Light, you know that man probably worked his ass off because he drank cheap beer once in his life.

Cheers has nothing on the World Famous Drift In - AMI, by the way. Nothing. It's just crazy shit. Dudes wear kilts and cowboy hats, rollin' in on a Vespa-like motorcycle with a side cart. And they are hanging with guys in Armani sunglasses and asking hey what can I give you today. People give around here in many ways. Yes, people give their bad times too, but that's part of the bar. The reason people are comfortable enough going through hard times there is because they know they are not going to be judged and they know there is someone in there that went through what they went through just on the other side of the bar.

People come in and ask "You got an espresso martini?" And I'm like no! This is a dive bar woman. We don't do shit like that. We don't have an espresso machine, we've got coffee. And that ain't gonna cut it because we don't have the right vodka to make it. You make them laugh and understand that the reason you are here is not because of espresso martini's but those people wake up very quickly and by the time they leave, they have a different perspective of the bar. I think it's awesome because they came in wanting an espresso martini and leave drinking a PBR and happy about it. Now that's a great bar.

THE LOCALS

What does it mean to be local on Anna Maria Island? Do you have to live on the island? Do you have to frequent the Drift In? Are those from Cortez Fishing Village locals? Who knows. I guess I would say a local at the Drift takes on new meaning. If this is your "spot", you live within the Sarasota/Bradenton area and this is the place you come to get away and be loved by many for who you are in the moment, then I guess you can consider yourself one of the locals.

So how do locals effect the World Famous Drift In - AMI you ask? Well that can be complex. As a customer I have one perspective and as a Bartender I have another. This is where understanding of thyself comes into play. Who we are in a moment will speak volumes for our approach not only to a situation but an overall agenda or attitude about life.

As a customer, my expectations are different than when I am slinging drinks like Nolan Ryan serving up a fast ball. As a customer my standard is pretty low. Acknowledge I am there, be polite, make a tasty cocktail, provide me with some intellect, and let's have some fun is all I expect.

Now as a Bartender, I expect some common sense. I am working my ass off and always striving to bring you the same expectation of myself as a customer, so don't be rude and come all up in here demanding service ahead of others. You might be special to your mama but you're not special to me. Just kidding. You can wait your turn like everyone else. I won't lie, my friends and locals usually get a little favoritism though. I might take their drink order first or give them a hug before I notice you. I do try my hardest to share my universal love and acceptance to all but I love my tribe. So suck it up buttercup. Yeah I learned that from my time in the US Navy as a Hospital Corpsman from 1994-1999. What a ride that was. Talk about tribe mentality, the military is a great example of that with the tribe being the United States of America baby. No boundaries on race, gender, religion, or any other bullshit title the government uses to divide us in the civilian world today. My Shipmates all stood side by side regardless of our differences for the greater good of defending the United States with our lives. Much respect to all my brothers and sisters I served with. Love you all. Shout out to my Boy Lt. Commander Dominic Romanowski who I met so many years ago and remains one of my closest friends to this day. We were both E nothings when we were on active duty together. I chose to get out get of the Navy and pursue my Bachelors of Science in K-12 Physical Education from Boise State University and my Masters of Education in Administration and Supervision from the University of Phoenix.

If anyone knows tribe, it is me. When you're thrown into foster homes and rely on strangers for safety it is imperative you learn survival skills at a young age in order to prep you for the battles you face through life. The reason I am able to thrive and understand the local mentality is because I don't see it, as I live here; therefore I am a local. I am a local because of the way I carry myself amongst strangers, not the proximity to the island. After all we are all here on earth as visitors so we are all locals on a more macro scale. Locals are key here at the Drift as they bridge the gap for tourists, island dwellers, and snowbirds alike. They are a vital role in showing all those who come from other places the warm hospitality that Anna Maria Island offers.

Meet Patty. She's a long time local who loves the World Famous Drift In – AMI. When asked about her experience here, this is what she said.

World Famous Drift In – AMI, aka "HEADQUARTERS", The Best Dive Bar Ever!

Sure we all have had a local bar in our lives that we frequented. I guess depending on where you call home might dictate your preferences for your favorite pour house. For me, well I moved to this little island from Los Angeles a dozen years ago. LA is quite the place for debauchery, celeb sightings, hobnobbing with the so-called elite for sure. I just threw up in my mouth a little writing that but...that is the criteria for anyone that wants to claim that they have been to the best bars around. Well, not so fast! The Drift has all that and more. Regardless of big city life of your financial status, if you are a Gen Xer like me, you are probably more likely to prefer the little dive on the corner to the big-time hot spot, or the place where all the "cool kids" hang out. And maybe we are not the first to refer to our local drinking hole as "HQ" but our local little bar is indeed, Headquarters and here's why.

I've been in there with Celebs; I've sat next to wealthy. I've taken in some exceptional music. Shit, I've sat next to homeless and even the beyond drunkards. I've danced with ex-athletes. I've seen fights break out. I've watched wedding parties come through and recently I swear there was even an unconfirmed sighting of a current champion head coach a couple of weeks ago in there. I still think it was him LOL. I've been in there in my swimsuit and cover up, been in there sunburned and sandy. I've been dressed to impress, dead sober and sloppy drunk. It's all good, every bit of it is accepted, expected and welcomed. If you look up the definition of headquarters it reads, "The place or building serving as the managerial and administrative center of an organization." This little organization called AMI knows very well that the Drift is the heartbeat of this island. It's where the local flavor and the tourist worlds collide. It's where for my tribe anyhow, many important decisions and happenings take place. Meetings, romance, birthdays, celebrations of life. It's the conference room for sure. When you walk in it's a good 30 minutes of moving through the crowded space having to stop to greet your people because I guarantee, THEY ARE ALL THERE. I know they must leave at some point, but I don't know when because they are ALWAYS

Drifting (that's what we refer to hanging at the Drift.) It's like a never-ending party for those of us who have decided to call AMI home. But one that doesn't get old. 8:00 AM on a Saturday, midnight on a Sunday, it breathes. Lots of circles hang out there. Us, we go by "Oceans 8 " and our HQ is most definitely the Drift. Legend has it, once owned by "The Babe" and now belonging to the people of AMI. Just doesn't get any weirder, cooler and better.

Oceans 1

THE SNOWBIRDS & PART TIMERS

It takes a good mix of residents and visitors to make AMI what it is. In our opinion, there is no better place to be a "bird" than here. With no shortage of sunshine, beaches, food, shopping and fun, a place like this is where everyone wants to be, especially in the winters. Sorry friends, I know AMI is supposed to be the best kept secret, but word has gotten out!

As owner of AMI Radio, I had the privilege of hearing a lot of songs written about our beloved island. But when it comes to snowbirds, my buddies The Fungies, Mark Kerr and Gary Lindblom, said it best. Goes a little something like this:

Driving home from the beach late last night.
We couldn't turn left and we couldn't turn right.
Stuck behind another snowbird car.
The next three months that's where we are.
Chorus: We got snow birds all over the place.
Snow birds all over the place.

We got snow birds all over the place.

It's that time of year again.

They drive big Cadillacs, Lincolns too.

I even saw one in a Subaru.

They got minivans and SUVs.

Every damn one pulled out in front of me.

Chorus:

They come from New York, Canada too.

I even saw a plate from Kalamazoo.

Maryland, Kentucky and Tennessee

Anna Maria Island is where they all wanna be.

Chorus

Can't get a burger at Skinny's or park at the Moose

We tried the Drift In but it's just no use.

No parking at the beach, Publix is packed.

Son of a bitch, there's that big Cadillac!

Chorus

You know we're just kidding, you're our friends too.

Even that guy in the Subaru.

We know you're good people so we'll behave,

But when you're heading north, we'll just

smile and wave!

Chorus

Again the Drift attracts snowbirds to spring breakers and everyone in between. Many of our Drift friends have second homes here. And we love that several times throughout the year, we get to see their familiar faces and spend a little time together. One of these friends of ours who has a second home here and vacation rental properties finds The World Famous Drift In – AMI her favorite watering hole and here's why.

Meet Michelle

Ohhh, The Drift In!!! She keeps me coming back. And someday very soon, I will be a "permanent local," not a part time local. I came to the island about 25 years ago and found my way down Bridge Street to this cool little bar that reminded me of a bar back home in Wisconsin. I even found new friends there from my home town area in

WI. They too had just recently discovered Bradenton Beach's secret well.

Fast forward ten years. For one of our trips, I decided to introduce my husband to this area along the Gulf that had pulled at my heart, but I only visited every few years. The Drift was one of our first stops (and probably our last each night) and the next thing you know, we are buying a big rental on the Bay front, only a block off Bridge Street...how convenient! And yes, being one block away from the Drift at 1AM was a main factor in choosing this property!

The Drift In could be labeled as "The Best Dive Bar on the Island" but from where we are from, that is a coveted title. To earn the DIVE BAR title doesn't mean you are the worst bar; it just means the bar may not be as high-end in terms of décor or expectations, i.e. the restrooms, which actually has always passed my 2 second inspection. It exudes friendliness, fun times and sometimes adventures too fun to repeat (even though I know there are videos somewhere between my phone and my best friend, Crystal's phone that could definitely be YouTube worthy!) I can't tell you how many "best nights ever" we have had at the Drift.

My husband and I are bar owners as well. We own a retired golf course bar/banquet hall property in Wisconsin and we would be honored to carry the coveted title of dive bar, but our property is newly remodeled. The vibe a person gets from the Drift In is that of a dive bar. It comes from a great, personable Bartender that hustles yet makes the bar patrons feel like neighbors, you know, like sitting next to "Norm from Cheers". Whether it's one round or 10 rounds of happy hour libations. I could name about ten bars around the country that could qualify for the best local bar title and the Drift In would be in the top three.

When I first heard that the Drift was a popular stop for Sunday motorcycle rides, I knew this was my kind of bar. I have owned and ridden Harley Davidson's most of my life and knew I could find friends at this bar. To this day, I still stay in touch with a few of these brothers from years past. What I find great about this bar today is that you can still walk in and find a group of motorcycle riding friends and at the same time, sit down next to vacationers enjoying a week off from their crazy office schedules.

At the Drift In, we are all on VACA...like "Mannie, who has been on permanent vacation since who knows when. She's always there to greet you with a smile and a "pretty outfit". Even though she may fill out the shirts better than I, stop in and judge for yourself. I'm not sure how many years she has been there, but she is surely a Drift In Icon!

Every day you will hear a Newbie Drifter state "This is the best bar ever!" Sitting next to their beer-drinkin buddies laughing, dancing and drinking the night (or day) away.

That's how we all end our perfect days in paradise. Like they all say "We don't always plan to go to the Drift, but we always end up there!"

THE TOURIST

Anna Maria Island thrives on tourism. Nearly three million visitors come each year from all over the world in search of that island feel. And why not, AMI ranks in the top islands in the country year after year. This place is perfect for anyone who loves being near the water. Over the years, we have met many first time visitors to the area. Here is a poem of one we call Smiley. He is a fine example of the statement, not all who wander are lost.

Meet Tommy

I ventured from Oklahoma
looking for a new start
where everybody didn't know my name
I found that starting line in Cortez, Florida.
Zero people in all of Manatee county knew
my name or my story.

With the new beautiful feeling of being
anonymous I hopped on my long board
Headed toward the island, my straw hat,
fanny pack with my journal and speaker
playing Donavon Frankenreiter, searching
for a bar top open spot that needed me and
I needed it.
After I crossed over the Cortez Bridge, bound for
the beach front, I found a few stops with a
view and ice cold beer.
Looked good but my people weren't there.
Back on the board I drift down Gulf Drive to
Bridge Street.
To my enjoyment, I cruised up to my new
bar top home the Drift In.
Sometimes you just know.
Cash only and Busch Lights.
This place could only get better.
Better is exactly what happened.
The next 5 months went by fast in time.
The moments slow enough to drift in.
My head unable to forget.
Bar fun!
You put your money down, find The "Rock",

Kid "Rock", "Stone" Cold, "Rock" 'N' Roll,
Hard as a "Rock", then wait and see if you
win.

You rooted for your neighbors sitting at the
tiki bar top, a win would get a round of
Jello Shots.

I only saw victory one time, but the person next to me
won over 25 times.

Some may call me a lucky charm
I was just happy to be there.

When the sun went down I would head inside.

It was a different world with the same people.

My quarter rolling skills, dancing with the
live bands, and karaoke singing was my vibe.

Everything I did was taken with full acceptance.

The people of the Drift were my people.

Their cares were left at Bridge Street.

They had no judgment as they came from
all different experiences, they just wanted a good time.

The Drift In is where Smiley found his new name.

CHAPTER 6

EXTRAORDINARY CREW MEMBERS

Becoming a Bartender at the World Famous Drift In - AMI is not just an occupation; it's an initiation into a distinguished league of libation wizards who have engaging personalities. Only a select few, possessing an alchemical blend of charisma, skill, and a knack for reading the room, earn the coveted opportunity to stand behind the bar that has witnessed countless tales unfold. Many vie for the chance, but only the exceptional make the cut, as the Drift In seeks not just Bartenders but maestros who can orchestrate an atmosphere of good cheer. Those who embark on this journey find themselves not just employees, but integral members of a tight-knit family, drawn by the magnetic charm of the Drift In. It's not merely a job; it's a commitment to crafting experiences, pouring spirits, and becoming part of the living legend that defines this world-famous establishment. In a place where only the best thrive, our Bartenders are the architects of unforgettable nights and the guardians of the Drift In's timeless legacy.

And it all starts with Doreen.

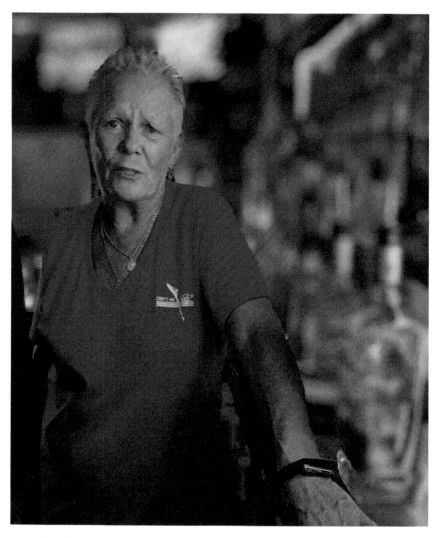

Anybody that's come in here, no matter what level of the community, resident or visitor, they know Doreen. She's got a heart of gold. It's all the intangibles that make her. First, she knows the people and understands the business. That woman has a big heart and she genuinely cares about people and the people she works with. She's honest to a T. If you don't pull your weight, she's going to call you on it. And that's what she does for everybody and that's what she should do. If I don't pull my weight or if I mess something up, Doreen is very good about asking what happened, rather than why the fuck didn't you do this?

We know that and she can handle herself too. And don't steal Mannie's wig, because Doreen will hunt you down and make you feel like shit until you pull it out of a purse with no pride left coming out of your soul.

She's been there over 28 years. Let's go back and have a look at how she came into the picture.

When Joe first came to own the bar, he had a manager there who he had an idea was stealing him blind. This was before he had cameras. So Joe paid what's called a Squatter to come in and be his eyes. He paid him to come in for an hour, have a drink or two and watch the cash register to make sure everything is going into the register. According to Joe, later this manager threw a Christmas party. She invited everyone from the bar to come over to her house. The place was packed with about 125 people and she was giving away free drinks. All of which he learned came from the Drift. She stole from Joe and the Squatter confirmed it. So Joe got rid of her and in walks Doreen.

She was a terrific Bartender and he soon made her the manager. At the time, Joe owned both the Drift In on Cortez and the Drift In on Anna Maria Island. Joe couldn't be at both places at one time. He trusted Doreen with his bar and his life. She's been there ever since.

She knows everything that works and doesn't work. She is very open minded. To Derek and Dan's credit, they listen to Doreen. Her input will always be there.

Here's a story about her loving nature and kindness. It really touched my heart when she took the time to come to the hospital and visit with me and brought me flowers .

It took me a while to figure out Doreen as a customer there. From the first time she took my drink order I could see how she operated. I could tell she's been doing the job for awhile. She moved with the elegance of a peacock and with the swiftness and strategy of 007. At times she even roared like a lion. But then again, I was also very high. I may or may not have had some brownies and smoked some pot an hour before throwing myself at the Drift In for the first time, but for you sober folks, she is fast, furious and always accurate.

After three years as a customer and now as a Bartender under her mentor-ship, she is unaware of how much I look up to her, not only as a Bartender, but a boss, a philanthropist, a loving, kind, and just person. Most of all, she's a friend. I think she always tries to do the right thing for the most benevolent outcome. She knows even if she has to be hard on someone, she does it with the right heart every single time. Cheers Doreen!!

~

As customers, we like to remember the Bartenders of the past including Jill, Jill and Jill, Sharon, Adam, Steve, Tiara and Angie. Current crew members consist of Amanda, Ashley, Melissa, Big Sexy, Tish, Debi and Heather.

Ahoy pirates, the crew at the Drift In is here to welcome you, to make sure your experience here is dive bar worthy and that you get home safely so you can return as a customer in the future.

DRIFT CREW MEMBERS CHRISTMAS 2023

CHAPTER 7

UNSPOKEN RULES

It's no secret that every bar has a spoken and unspoken code or etiquette that exists to keep things running smoothly and efficiently while keeping everyone safe and providing a good time. The Drift In is no different. We would suggest, just don't be an asshole and you'll be fine.

I'm going to go out on a limb when I say that most, if not all Bartenders have absolute pet peeves that drive them nuts when they are crowded. I think I speak for every Bartender there when I say there are certain dos and don'ts, speaking specifically for the Drift In. The first thing I feel that's worth mentioning is because of the leadership of Derek, Dan and Doreen, the staff feels very comfortable for being allowed to make decisions as a whole because we are backed by this awesome management team.

Here are some tips on the Drift's etiquette. Sometimes they are right in front of you. Just know the customer is not always right here. That sets the tone for the staff to be just in their decision making because we know if we kick somebody out, we lose their business so we don't take that decision lightly. But we also don't want to lose business at the cost of that person. As a private business who deals with a volume of people under the influence of alcohol, we feel it is important to keep the environment safe and if that means removing someone, then we will and even bar them if need be so they cannot come back. That is for the betterment of the community or the atmosphere of the Drift.

According to Joe Cuervo, a guy named Morgan is just one of many who have been permanently barred from the establishment. Joe tells the story of Morgan causing a ruckus more than once with the patrons at the bar, Joe stated he personally banned him. Now Morgan is a friend of ours and a well known member of the community and so we are definitely not bashing him. We love him and he often jokes about it himself. And it's funny that he still comes around the Drift, though now he must stay on the outside. But it's no surprise to find him out front visiting with a local or two. I often see Morgan when I'm working on my shift popping his head in to say hello to friends. Frickin funny though that he's not able to step inside.

Friends, don't let this happen to you!

For me personally as a Bartender, this is my criteria so we can all get along easily. Don't be an asshole, be patient, be open minded, lighthearted and be ready to have some fun with Big Sexy. And with that, we will all get something out of the experience.

Now, I'm about to tell you of a story of a lady you should not emulate.

Story goes like this. I got a full bar. I'm, busting my ass. I'm moving at a pace of a cheetah, with cat-like reflexes, moving customer to customer. Juggling 3-4 pints of beer at a time, hustling for ice water, Jello shots, Long Island iced teas, and then our eyes met. The lady with a stare from hell! She looks me straight in the face with direct eye contact, you can cut the tension with a knife, having the audacity to look me, Big Sexy, the ultimate customer service representative officianato. The dive bar concierge of concierges. Nah, I'm just fucking with you, but I am pretty good at customer service. It is at this point she tells me I'm ignoring her. Without hesitation I say, are you kidding me? And she looked back at me with laser eyes like she wanted to burn my very soul. I felt she wanted to turn me into a pile of ashes. And then she states, my husband had to go in and get our drinks. Once again, without hesitation, I say if you are not happy with the service, you can leave lady, because the customer is not always right. Needless to say she had no response and she and her husband enjoyed sitting at the bar for a couple hours, where I served them and we had no further issues. I even received a tip. So you see the Drift In has a way of waking people up with their behaviors.

Top 5 Pet Peeves

#5 People talking to me while I'm counting money.

#4 Not knowing what you want when ordering.

#3 Asking me for just a cup of ice.

#2 Asking me for a glass of water while I have a full bar.

   Waiting for the nectar of the gods (booze).

#1 Don't call me Paul when Big Sexy's in the house.

Ladies: Well I walked into the bathroom and I thought for a moment that they finally removed that stenchy bathroom smell it's always had, but then I thought, I could just be used to the smell, as it is a home away from home.

Men: Why the fuck can only one dude be in the bathroom at a time when you have a urinal and a commode? And please fellas, stop picking your noses and wiping your boogers on the wall above the men's urinal. It's quite disgusting, but I also understand as a man who has traveled through many towns and many bars that this is a common practice amongst the Neanderthals who urinate in the same facilities that I do. And I feel that's just disgusting. Come on, you know you guys are in tune enough to know better. Please if you decide to take a shit, do not use the paper towels that we dry our hands with and try to flush those down with island plumbing being what it is, it makes for pretty shitty scene. Now that's just for the bathroom.

I once read a quote on the bottom of a Mickey's bottle top that said, "Squirtle: The reason why people wear shoes in public restrooms." Ladies and gentlemen, if you choose to walk around the Drift In barefoot, do not sue us for any mental damages you will sustain from people making fun of you for your jiffy mart feet, compliments of the floor at the Drift In. I see people walk in there barefoot all the time, it's disgusting. I mean I'm not going to lie, the floor needs some work, it's an old bar, but that's what people love about it. We love the fact it is that way. "It's Drifty."

So here's the deal people, I know you are paying customers but use some common sense and please don't stand where the Bartenders and bar backs are constantly walking back and forth between bars. I really don't wanna have to sick TJ on your ass.

So let me fill you in on TJ. He is as raw as they come, filterless, fearless, and in his own way, very kind and will do anything he can to make your life easier. For that he is so appreciated for the job that he does as bar back. But don't let all that kindness fool you because if you step out of line, he'll make sure you get back in line his way and that might not go the way you want it to, but we all know he has our back. Feel free when you see TJ to buy that dude a nonalcoholic Heineken Zero because he deserves it and he will make sure you're safe and have a great time while you're visiting.

For your parking needs, the Drift has hired some of the very finest parking lot attendants on the planet. Two that come to mind are Marty, rest in peace. Most people think he was a big asshole. But those who got to know Marty would say he was our kind of asshole and we loved him for it. You might ask who was Marty? He was a one legged grouchy guy riding around on a scooter, who may have been found yelling at customers to get their cars straightened out and properly directing traffic. That was his job. He was family to those who got to know him a little bit.

And today we have Jerry. He is the antithesis of Marty. He has a calm demeanor who also properly directs traffic and is definitely appreciated.

The parking lot rules are as follows. You are free to park in the parking lot taking up only one space as long as you are at the Drift drinking responsibly. Along the same lines, stop arguing with the Bartenders and the staff members when we try to stop you from driving away while you're intoxicated. We are just looking out for you and want everybody in the community to be safe to return back to drink like the legends we are.

And here's the deal if you're gonna use our parking lot, don't block customers in while you leave the facility. Then you return to bitch about your car being towed away and for the record if we're gonna get technical, you know we've called for you at least three times. A commotion has been made for the person who's being blocked by you and you were not here so don't say it's our fault. Hold yourself accountable and go pay the $300-500 it's gonna be to get out of the tow yard, but thanks for coming. See you next time!

The last of the unspoken rules is and please the only thing you must do is cover your nipples. Because really that's the only thing. Women can come in a bikini. Men can show up with an unbuttoned shirt. But, no matter what your nipples have to be covered!

CHAPTER 8

MANNIE

Mannie - she stands 5'6" and 116 lbs. 80 of which lie in her breasts. She's slutty to nutty to beautiful. She's festive. She's sexy. She is MANNIE. She never moves. She never speaks. Her figure is always on point. She is the only woman every man's woman would allow for some flirtatious fun. Don't worry ladies, she loves your attention as well. The way she gets fondled in the bar by these strange guys who come in and have the need to feel her up and grope her, take pictures of her, sniff her, steal her wig and that kind of shit.

This mannequin with the vivacious appearance is a Drift Icon and perhaps an island Icon. Joe Hendricks, local reporter for the AMI Sun, a great drummer, and patron to the Drift who you will meet in the next chapter, wrote a great article about Mannie a few years back and it is worthy of being a part of this book.

In an article by Joe Hendricks for the AMI Sun:

BRADENTON BEACH – After a brief absence, Mannie the mannequin is back at the Drift In.

Over the past decade or so, five different mannequins have served as the Bradenton Beach establishment's lifelike female mascot. Mannie 5.0 debuted in early January after her predecessor was damaged beyond repair in late 2018.

"I came in after Halloween and she was missing an arm, a hand and she had three broken fingers. It was impossible to fix. I've fixed other ones over the years, but that one was totally trashed," Drift In manager Doreen Flynn said.

Unable to find a replacement online, Flynn pieced a new Mannie together using parts from her own mannequin and spare and salvaged parts saved over the years.

Late last year, a Drift In patron broke off some of the previous Mannie's fingers. – Joe Hendricks | Sun

"This mannequin is actually mine and I'm donating it back to the bar, but it's the last one. I tried to replace her and I couldn't. That's not even her real leg. I bonded it with epoxy and you wouldn't even know it unless you lift up her dress, which some people do. I used red duct tape to make it look like a garter and I put the garter over it. I glued both hands on and someone made her some fake bracelets," Flynn said of her handiwork.

Mannie 5.0 is accompanied by the new sign that says, "Please do not move our Mannie. Photos Only! We have tried to replace her, they do not make her anymore."

Regarding the sign, Flynn said, "That's the last Mannie, that's why I wrote this sign. Martha Kelley's going to make a nice one for me and I'm going to frame it. I'm asking all our customers to help me and keep an eye on her because she just can't be replaced. She's our Mannie."

Flynn also reflected on the tribulations suffered by previous Mannies.

"One time, her hands went missing and I found them next door at the Sports Lounge – somebody was drumming on the bar with them. A couple years ago, one of her legs got broken off when somebody picked her up and tried to dance with her. I took the leg to the hardware store and the man thought I was going to make the leg lamp from 'A Christmas Story,'" Flynn said.

Someone is now making Flynn a leg lamp using a previous mannequin's leg.

The origins of Mannie

"It was my husband's idea. Years ago, he had one in his bar," Flynn said of Mannie's origins.

Flynn shared the idea with Drift In owner Joe Cuervo and asked if he'd buy a mannequin. Cuervo said yes and the legend of Mannie was born.

"Everybody loved it. People would bring in their own clothes. They changed her for football games and different holidays. It's been a smashing success. She's the most photographed woman on the island and she's known all over the world," Flynn said.

In 2015, Mannie wore this costume for Halloween. Joe Hendricks | Sun

"The first time I brought Mannie in I didn't tell anybody. I had the seat down in my car and all you could see was this perfect body with a sheet over it. The first night, I

put her by the end of the bar and it startled everyone, so we found this spot for her," Flynn said of Mannie's traditional place between the back door and the package to go cooler.

BeachHouse chef Donald White carried the original Mannie into the bar.

"That was at least 10 years ago. The cops watched us carrying a body and asked what it was," he recalled.

"Mannie looks good. She's more popular than ever and loving life," White said of the new Mannie.

Fashion plate

Every week or so, Flynn changes Mannie's outfit, hairstyle and hair color and her ever-changing appearance adds to the mystique. Some outfits are work-like and conservative, others are revealing and risqué. As Hurricane Irma approached in 2017, Mannie donned a lifejacket.

In 2017, a Drift In patron named L.J. shared Mannie's concerns about the threat Hurricane Irma posed to Anna Maria Island. – Doreen Flynn

Local business owner and Anna Maria Island Chamber of Commerce board of directors chairperson Bev Lesnick appreciates Mannie's photographic nature and social media presence.

"It's a good Instagram, Facebook or Pinterest picture. Mannie is known worldwide," Lesnick said.

"I think Mannie gives men hope," her friend Amy Tobin joked.

"When you walk in and see Mannie you know you're at the Drift. If you don't know Mannie, you're not a local," said Seafood Shack Bartender Delanie Herlihy-Kos.

"Mannie has feelings too," Kos said to those who might mean her harm.

Bradenton Realtor Andy Cochran became a Mannie fan back when he still split his time between Florida and Vermont.

"She's the main attraction of Bridge Street for me. She keeps me coming back. After recovering from her plastic surgery, she's just as beautiful as ever. Welcome back Mannie," he said.

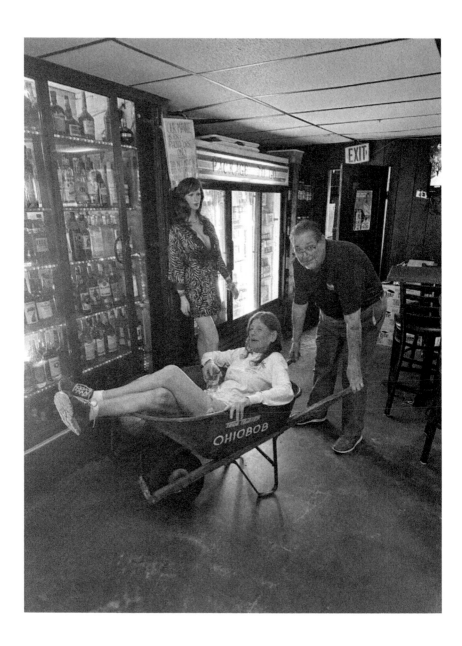

CHAPTER 9

TIMELESS ENTERTAINMENT

Ask yourself what it is you look for in a bar that keeps you coming back time after time. Is it the people? Is it the staff? The ambiance? The bands? Or is it the fun games you can play? Well the Drift In has it all! Some of the best musicians, eccentric characters that perch themselves at the top of the bar stools, the wittiness of the game hosts or cool ass Bartenders. The liveliness of it all. This is some of the entertainment you can find at the World Famous Drift In-AMI.

- Live Music
- Bingo
- Trivia
- Karaoke
- Bar Fun

Check out the current calendar. Subject to change.

DRIFT-IN AMI

WEEKLY EVENTS!

MONDAY
Bingo: 1pm – 5pm
Card Games: 530pm – 8pm
Live Music: 9pm – 1am (Tommy B)

TUESDAY
Card Games: 530pm – 8pm
Trivia: 7pm – 9pm
Karaoke: 9pm – 1am

WEDNESDAY
Bingo: 1pm – 5pm
Card Games: 530pm – 8pm
Live Music: 9pm – 1am (Steve Paradis)

THURSDAY
Bingo: 1pm – 5pm
Card Games: 530pm – 8pm
Live Music: 9pm – 1am (Dos Macs)

FRIDAY
Live Music: 1pm – 5pm (Dos Macs)
Card Games: 530pm – 8pm
Live Music: 9pm – 1am

SATURDAY
Live Music: 2pm – 6pm (Outside)
Card Games: 530pm – 8pm
Live Music: 9pm – 1am (Inside)

SUNDAY
Live Music: 2pm – 6pm (Tommy B – Outside)
Card Games: 530pm – 8pm
Karaoke: 9pm – 1am

www.driftinami.com

Bingo at the Drift is absolutely one of the greatest shit shows on the island. It brings a cast of characters that are sure to sharpen your wit. An anything goes motto applies and people are sure to take a polar plunge into the world of sexual innuendo, political correctness, superiority complexes, and so much more at every opportunity. I mean when O 69 is called no less than ten people will surely have some remark but none other than my favorite "who's hungry" comes flying out of someone's mouth. I mean come on people have some couth. This is the Drift baby and you better bring your A game if you want to shine at bingo. Trust me there are people that believe that this is their moment. Some people have sports, some have money, fame, or they may even be top dog at their job. But they are definitely not as cool as Bar Bingo Guy on BINGO days. I mean this is BINGO baby. Where the dirtier and wittier you appear, the more people aspire to be like you in that moment.

Personally I like the game top or bottom. I mean who wouldn't want their choice. The lazy lover in all of us pick bottom. Just kidding there are two ways to win BINGO across the bottom or the top never including the free space. Poor free space, you're out this game but you might get your chance in the next game.

This is a far cry from how I was brought up in the BINGO system and why maybe Bingo at the Drift means something nostalgic to me. You see after the foster homes, my loving aunt Joanne and uncle Fred had taken me in to live with them. My aunt was the greatest thing on earth for many reasons but we are talking BINGO here so let's stay relevant. She began taking me to bingo at a very young age when I had been suspended from school usually for fighting. If I were to guess I would have to say around eight years old. I remember the smoke filled gas chamber like BINGO halls, usually at a church or temple. Could you imagine being eight years old fresh out of foster homes where you have been tossed around for years and have seen so many places and faces and now find yourself amongst some of the crankiest old ladies yelling and screaming at everything from where's my coffee, whistling woot whew at O sixty nine, combing my hair and telling my aunt how cute I was, to screaming at the caller, slow down. I mean these ladies and yes back in the early eighties BINGO was dominated by really creepy, angry, and horny women. This not so much the case today as society has been waging war on men for years and many today have emasculated themselves into pansies who play BINGO regularly. Myself being one of those so yeah I can say pansy. Man I had a messed up childhood for sure, but it has prepared me for what transpires at work as I bartend two days of BINGO.

So after years of observing these Bingoholics my aunt thought it would be awesome to start allowing me to play my very own BINGO cards and I mean that shit was kinda cool for a little kid. You mean I can win money and you are buying me in. That's awesome! So now here I am ten maybe eleven years old and the designated church or temple has no issue that I am playing BINGO for MONEY. I mean was gambling even legal in New York back in the eighties? Is it legal for someone my age to be gambling back then? You know the orphaned boy now under age gambling in a religious establishment kind of thing. I'm sure you get the point. I remember when I was twelve I got my huge break in the BINGO nation. My aunt got me a job or made me a slave to the temple, either way I was cool with it. It meant I was gonna make some coin and I was down for that. I only worked for tips and twenty bucks was twenty bucks. That's about what I made a night in tips. Plus free food, shit I was gold especially from where I came from. So yes this makes me a BINGO expert. Therefore I know BINGO guy when I see one.

~

Now let's talk karaoke where neither Big Sexy nor Casey thrive but enjoy playing along.

This is not your ordinary karaoke bar. The talent here is unbelievable. Every Sunday and Tuesday night, the Drift fills with unsuspecting folks about to surprise the shit out of you. First we gotta talk about Kelly. This amazing, beautiful, hard working woman is so passionate about music. Her natural singing ability will wow any person in the room. Whether she's singing Bon Jovi or the Starred Spangled Banner, she brings the room to a sudden halt to listen. So powerful. Every person in the room can't help but have goosies as they feel her song.

Now let's talk about the other singers. You may know some of them. Let's say TJ for example. The Drift In's bar back. Tattooed from head to toe, you'd never know how nice, hardworking and talented of a guy he really is when he is at his best. You gotta give props to this guy. Why? He has bounced around as a cook at almost every establishment on the island. And since he has given up alcohol, he has been working at the Drift. We have watched this guy grow his singing voice over time. From old country to today's alternative rock, his baritone sound is rich and unique. He's even sang with locals Dos Macs. Now you have the majestic Laurie Lancaster. I, Paul, personally enjoy listening to my wife Laurie sing. When I watch her voluptuous body in motion and hear her angelic voice, not only do the hairs on my neck stand up but it is then that "it" moves.

Laurie captures the emotions of patrons when she sings her rendition of Ave Maria in Latin. Her operatic voice often brings people to tears as it triggers emotions and fantasy. She can sing any range from Pink to Pavarotti. So now we finished with a couple of the fantastical singers, you get everyone from Big Sexy singing Tequila, even missing one of the verses. To the drunken, stumbling bridal parties who come in with the utmost confidence thinking they can sing Christina Aguilera or they can shine like Lady Gaga. They end up sounding like Christina Snagulera and they shine like a fake zirconia. They make our ears ring and not in a good way, but we love their effort and commitment to authentically sucking. If you're reading this and it describes you, take a bow because we love you.

Newcomers, if you feel so inclined to join in on karaoke night, do as I would do and pick your song choices wisely. You want songs with hardly any words such as Tequila, but don't be stealing my song, or have at it and pick something like Sweet Caroline where everyone will join in to help you. And that's how you'll find success at karaoke night at the Drift. Even if you suck at singing!

Now for Bar Fun, which happens nightly. We have the strapping lad named Terry who loves his momma and happens to be one of Big Sexy's closest friends on the island. He has a heart of gold and the warmest smile and a gentle touch. But don't be fooled. He's 6'3" with a mohawk sculpted by "Sexay" hair gel, giving him a most distinct look. His guns are blazing because the sun shines down on his sleeveless arms. He moves with grace as he deals cards to patrons. If you're Doyle Brunson or Phil Ivey, this isn't your typical card game, so chill out and give Terry a break. He's just dealing cards! It's not like Terry can tell you what cards are coming up next as we have twenty plus incomplete decks to deal.

Every Tuesday, we shift to the "know it alls" giving them space to flourish. There are fun honest people, those who google and cheat, trivia at the Drift truly brings out the best and worst in people. My friends used to tell me if I wasn't cheating, I wasn't trying and my response was always the same. "It isn't worth winning if I have to cheat." So do us all a favor. Stop using your phones when playing trivia! It's just a game. Come and have fun. Buy some drinks. Socialize. Nobody cares who wins. Here are three types of teams we usually see group up.

1.   I don't give a fuck team. Which usually consists of a bunch of people who have already had a few to drink who don't care if they win or lose. And they will play honestly. They love to just have some laughs and entertainment and possibly win a free drink.

2.   The Yin-Yang team. Half of which are in it to win it at all costs. The other half don't give a shit, they just enjoy being part of the team. This team you gotta keep an eye on though because the competitive ones might sneak a peak at their phone.

3.   The Trivia Nazis. The know it all group. Sure to be

some inter-group dynamics that affect judgment in their answers. So the probability of cheating goes up as they have so many good answers that they need one definitive answer.

Let's dance on over to the music scene. As you may or may not have heard by now, the music here is deep and talented and has a loyal following. While this area is rich in musical talent, playing at the World Famous Drift In – AMI is for a select few. They have the bands they like and you are lucky to get a spot playing here otherwise. It's a common thread for patrons and performers to have an affection for this little dive bar on Bradenton Beach.

Getting to know some of the musicians on a personal note has been a huge advantage to me for my own personal growth. Not only does their music speak to me, but it touches my soul. A few musicians I would like to mention who I've gotten to know a little about personally are Concrete Edgar, Cabana Dogs, Rob Hamm, Steve Paradis and Tommy B. I look forward to a growing relationship with all these individuals as they bring value to my life just by knowing them, listening to their music and watching them do what they love.

~

Over the years, I've had an opportunity to get to know nearly all of the musicians that play here. Several have been a part of either AMI Radio or Real Island TV. As a girl who loves good music and dancing, this is the place for it. Don't be fooled by this little bar, it packs a punch when it comes to getting down on the dance floor. We don't mind scrunching in to get our groove on around here.

~

Don't take our word for it. There is this vibe or vortex around the Drift that is better being experienced. Here are some of the musicians to tell you of their love for this establishment.

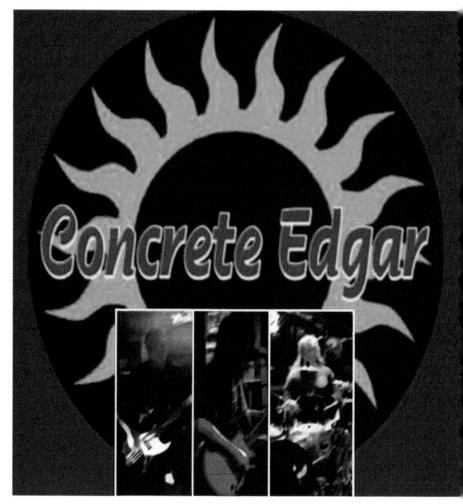

CONCRETE EDGAR - @concreteedgar

I'm Mikey Silbaugh. I am the singer/guitarist/songwriter
for the band Concrete Edgar. Concrete Edgar is a rock
power trio consisting of myself, Tom Fioretti
(Bass/Vocals), and Joe Freed (Drums/Vocals). Our band
is modeled around bands like Gov't Mule, Rush, and of
course Led Zeppelin. We pride ourselves on how

passionate and particular we are on our choice of music and how we present it. It is not just classic rock (unfortunately now days practically all rock is classic rock). It is Jam Band interpretations and us leaning quite heavily on our Prog influences. Every night is a different show. Well… except for set 2; our featured "power hour" medley of songs.

We have been playing at the Drift In since 2014. That was our very first gig as Concrete Edgar. Joe and I started a year earlier with my sister Patti Brainard. Patti was actually who booked the band at the venue in the beginning. The Drift gig was our first in many ways as a band. It was also the place of Patti's final full performance before her passing in 2014. She loved the energy of the Drift so much so it was truly a blessing and fitting that was her final performance. We had just started gaining momentum. I will never forget how happy she was with every Drift gig.

To give credit where credit is due and there is A LOT of credit to give. Our friends make every show very special. We are all sharing in the same experience from different vantage points. From the deep voice, playful heckling of "play something we know!!!" to just sharing in our weird sense of humor. Some friends help make set decisions. I would call them "requests" but it is different when they know your 150 song list better than you do sometimes. LOL! They help non residents feel at home and welcome them into our little party. Our friends are the absolute greatest!!!! So much love!!!!

There have been so many fond moments at the Drift. I think our favorite moment, which got saved in time via a lovely picture, was our friend David as Santa Claus. Every year he and his wife Martha would be Mr. and Mrs. Claus. They would park the sleigh in front of the Drift. We got on the sleigh as a band and had our picture taken with Santa. Just a beautiful holiday moment.

We love the Drift, it has been our base gig for 9 years now. It is always the best gigs of the month for us. Deliberately or naturally, big or small something special always happens for us there. A laugh that the 3 of us can't seem to let rest. The bar packed with people dancing. A solo that is really vibing that night. The bass and drums driving so hard like a semi speeding down the highway. On a night when we aren't playing there, there are a huge amount of uber talented people booked at the Drift. We are very proud to be in the same line up with bands/people that we are fans of! Thank you for giving us the opportunity to create music for you.

ROB HAMM – RobHammLive.com

My name is Rob Hamm. My band is Rob Hamm & the Daily Specials. I called the band that because I never knew who I was playing with from week to week. The island has so much musical talent. I've been blessed to play with the musicians I've met since I started playing in this area. Gregg Allman and Aretha Franklin's bass players, Marvin Gaye's drummer, and so many other great seasoned professional musicians.

When I first started going to Drift In, it was mostly to drink and sing karaoke. I got to meet the local Drift In staples. We all really cared about each other while still taking the time to bust each others stones, if you will. A while after meeting guitarist/singer Tommy Balbo, he asked me to fill in for him at a few shows. Dos Macs would from time to time ask me to guest spot on Saturday days. Steve Paradis asked me to fill in. Eventually, after about a year of filling in for Tommy, and other acts that Doreen would call me in for, I was offered the first Friday of every month. Like I said earlier, blessed.

My favorite memory playing there has to be the benefit for Mack Black. Mack had undergone some health issues, missing shows, and racking up major medical bills. The island provided. Doreen messaged all of us to see who could possibly donate some time for a benefit. Everybody helped out. Koko Ray, The Cabana Dogs, Mikey Silbaugh from Concrete Edgar, my band and so many more. Lance Biddle from the 301 Travelers performed, provided the sound system, and auctioned off gift baskets. Even the regulars who won baskets were donating them back to raise more money. It was truly a community coming through to help one of their own. I love the Drift for so many reasons, but I'll never forget that day.

STEVE PARADIS - @stevenparadis

Hello all, my name is Steve Paradis. My days at the Drift predate when I started performing there by several years. I would go to enjoy live music, a football game, or just enjoy the company of many of the locals who would also frequent the establishment. It truly is like a family.

So when I was asked to perform there, it was truly a pleasure. I had stepped in with Dos Macs on occasion, or Concrete Edgar for instance, or covered for another performer who wasn't available, but then my tenure with "Tony da Band" gave me a steady gig there. Several years ago, I started performing solo on Wednesdays and it's one of my favorite gigs. The atmosphere is awesome, the staff is incredible and the patrons are nothing less than pure fun!

CABANA DOGS - @cabanadogsmusic

My name is Jimi C and I am in a band called The Cabana Dogs. The Cabana Dogs consist of myself on vocals and guitar, Kathy Packwood on vocals, Sean McCord on vocals and drums, and Willy D playing Bass guitar. We also sometimes have our percussionist Cajun and our good friend Jimmy Flower adding more vocals and rhythm guitar. We are an upbeat coastal rock band that loves to play at the World Famous Drift In - AMI. Our set list is comprised of hits that everyone knows spanning decades, done our own rocking way. As someone who has played everywhere, inside and outside of this country, I can say with confidence that the Drift In is my favorite place to play. So much so that we have written a few songs about the Drift and the island. One is called "Can't be the Rum" and the other is "Anna Maria". We have others referencing the area as well. We have also created custom soaps named after the island. I used to visit Anna Maria Island when I lived I NYC and for years would come here thinking that this is the most beautiful place. Now, many years later and many islands, resorts and stages later, I still hold it to be so. On Anna Maria there are many bars and restaurants, all with different types of food and entertainment. The place that always sticks out and has been here for decades is The Drift In on Bridge St. The Cabana Dogs play the Drift In once or twice a month and always have a great time. The crowd is straight forward about wanting to dance and sing along to great music. I love when the vacationers and the locals pour in and out like waves. The flow is exhilarating. At any given moment we are playing to a wedding party, several birthdays and a few family outings. This is a real, feet on the ground place. We feel at home here and so does the island. A few of my favorite moments are when Taylor Hicks, American Idol winner in season 5, came and sang with us while visiting the Drift In. Another is when Coach "Coop" from the Lightening came and let us drink from the Stanley Cup. You never know what's going to happen at the Drift In on Anna Maria Island. Half of our set list and mashups were learned and created while on stage playing at the Drift. It is place where we can try just about anything. The Cabana Dogs love to have our friends come up and do a song or two with us. All the bands that play here at the Drift are friends. It's like a little musical family. We all support each other and fill in for each other, and to top it off, it has some of the most beautiful beaches, and I've been on a lot of them.

JOE HENDRICKS - @joehendricksAMI

Joe Hendricks began playing band gigs at the Drift In in 2011. A year later, he wrote the first of many newspaper stories he's written about the Drift In as a reporter for the Anna Maria Island Sun.

"My first gig at the Drift In was with Ted Stevens and Charles Nardone. We were a relatively new rockabilly band at the time and we were still trying to get a foothold in the Bradenton Beach music scene. I remember people throwing money at us as we played that night and I've had many great and wild nights there in the years that have followed," Joe said.

"After the rockabilly band moved on to higher paying venues, I went several years without playing the Drift In, but I was still a regular patron. In January 2023, Dos-Macs lead guitarist/lead singer Mike McConnell asked me to be the drummer for the 'Heat in the Street' gigs that take place in the Drift In parking lot every Saturday afternoon from 2-6 p.m., weather permitting. With Mack Black on bass, vocals and harmonica, Rich Dugan on guitar and vocals and several other special guests that come and go, that's become a favorite gig of mine. I also play the Drift In regularly with the Zack Yoder Group and Tommy Balbo and The Collective," Joe said.

"The first story I wrote for the AMI Sun was about the Anna Maria Island Privateers' Grog tasting party that took place in the Drift In parking lot in 2012. I was there with camera in hand on St. Patty's Day, March 17, 2020, when all of Florida's stand-alone bars were ordered to close that day at 5 p.m. and remain closed until further notice as part of the Florida Governor Ron DeSantis' initial response to the COVID-19 pandemic. A few minutes after 5 p.m., I took a photo of Bartender Sharon Bell standing all alone behind a now-empty Drift In tiki bar that was jam-packed 10 minutes earlier," Joe said.

"I've written about numerous fundraising events the Drift In has hosted to assist and support local families and community members in need during the holidays and throughout the year. I've also written farewell stories about Drift In patrons and employees who've passed away, including patron Bob "Coop" Cooper and longtime employee David Marshall in 2021, parking lot attendant Marty Tupin in 2023 and Buddy Lee, the beloved neighborhood dog in 2018. I've also written about the trials and tribulations of the Drift In's ultra-sexy mascot, Mannie the Mannequin," Joe said.

"The Drift In is my favorite bar. It's the one place I can go on any night of the week and know that I'll run into at least one person I know. I'm proud to be a small part of the Drift In history and the extended Drift In family that includes management, staff, musicians and patrons all looking out for one another," Joe said.

TOMMY BALBO (TOMMY B) @tommybalbo

In an interview with Casey, Tommy said he's been playing at the Drift for 20+ years, possibly longer than any musician. He's brought a lot of people here to the Drift including Jimi C from The Cabana Dogs who originally to play bass with him. His band, Tommy B and the Collective has been a part of the Drift community both as a musician and patron. He loves that everybody knows his name. Though musicians have drifted in and out of Tommy's band, hc has stood the test of time.

DOS MACS - @mikemcconnell

In an interview with Casey, Mike McConnell recalls that he first came here to visit nearly 30 years ago and had been out on the pier fishing. At the time, he was living in Orlando. While walking by with his kids, he stuck his head into the Drift In and there was a guy there playing. He says he's noticed that often, as a dad doing just as he had done, poking their heads in with kids in tow, seeing what was going on at the Drift.

Mike started playing 12 years ago. He began singing at the Drift as a single act. That's actually when he and I met with AMI Radio. Mike was working at Island Time and would come and sit in with Koko Ray. Every time he got done at Island Time, just as so many musicians do, would come over to the Drift to play a little after hours. Then it got real, Doreen started scheduling him for dates and now of course, he's a staple.

Mike says what sets this place a apart from other bars is diversity. It was like this since he first walked in. Still today can be diverse. "I fell in love with this place a long time ago. You're not supposed to fall in love with a smoky little dive bar, but I did!"

There's just something about this little hole in the wall. It's home. It's our comfort zone." It's probably a little too easy to get comfortable around here.

Dos Macs can be found playing weekly both indoors and outside at the tiki!

As you can see, the music here is stellar. The quality of people that play at the Drift are definitely a part of what makes this place "Dive Bar Worthy" as Big Sexy would say. Not only do each of the bands and others play regularly here, they and many others, are more than happy to help support our Drift community when it comes to someone needing help. Over the years, this establishment has hosted many benefit concerts to help out and its no surprise, these talented folks donate their time to help raise some funds.

A special and more recent event actually went to help out Mack Black and they were able to raise over $7,000 for him when he was out sick and couldn't play.

So when you come to the Drift, stick around for the music and entertainment. There is no shortage of fun things and good times going around here. There really is something for anybody who loves to get out and about and have a damn good time!

CHAPTER 10

DRIFTING AND STUMBLING INTO THE FUTURE

What was once known as the best kept secret is out! Anna Maria Island will continue to be a top vacation destination in Florida for people of all ages. It has been written about in books, poetry and song. It's been featured on television, magazine and newspaper articles around the world. It is our hope that it will keep its "Old Florida" charm and natural beauty. The Drift In is as much a part of the island's history as it is one of the oldest establishments still thriving today with no signs of slowing down anytime soon.

As the Drift approaches its legendary 100 year anniversary the bar stools keep turning and the booze continues to flow, good times will be had by most, the quarters are still rollin and music is in the air. Currently the awesome crew members are slinging the best and cheapest "Dive Bar Worthy" cocktails on the island. So make your way to down to Bridge Street by either walking, biking, hopping on the Monkey Bus or Trolley, and make the World Famous Drift In – AMI a stop along the way. You are sure not to be disappointed. And come see me, Big Sexy.

I'm the guy who's either going to convince you or confuse you. Either way, I'll make sure your experience is authentic and memorable. After all, you are hanging out the Miva, Big Sexy. Insert laugh.

If you have family or friends visiting the area, come see me for the best island tour with Zegway by the Bay. It is guaranteed FUN! Thinking of doing a podcast or YouTube channel and don't know where to start? I'm the girl to call.

Stay tuned for the Drift In Stumble Out Show. And while you're here be sure to take a picture with the beautiful Mannie and post it to the Facebook page Drift In – AMI. Locals, don't forget to play your VIP numbers and if you don't know what that means, stop in and talk to one of the crew members on how to acquire a number and get details. And for you tourist and passers by, you won't want to miss this place. You may come as a stranger but you will leave as a friend and you will find this is the one and only place you can (without judgment) Drift In, Stumble Out.

The End

Find Out More

Casey Hoffman

    CaseyHoffmanPromotes.com

    ZegwayByTheBay.com

    RealIslandTV.com

Paul "Big Sexy" Weremecki

    SunriseHope.org

    Facebook.com/AMIDrumCircle

    YouTube.com/LoveLife4All

BE SURE TO FOLLOW US ON FACEBOOK AND ASK HOW TO BE A PART OF THE SHOW!

@DriftInStumbleOut

Printed in Great Britain
by Amazon

40483231R00086